Windows 1
2nd Edition

The Premiere User Guide for Work, Home & Play.

Cheat Sheets Edition: Hacks, Tips, Shortcuts & Tricks.

Standard Ordinary Human

Solutions & Training, 20-year Microsoft Veteran

Windows 10 for Beginners
2nd Edition

Release: 2.0.2.3c

Table of Contents

About Ordinary Human

Ordinary Human is a 20-year veteran of Microsoft who previously worked with various Microsoft teams to write documentation for Windows, Windows Server and other Microsoft products. If you have ever used any Microsoft product or operating system or had Microsoft training, you've probably seen Ordinary Human's work in action.

Ordinary Human pledges to update this manual from time to time to make corrections and changes as Windows 10 changes and to add content. How much time Ordinary Human can dedicate to the book depends on its readership and participation from readers like you.

1. Introduction

When it comes to technology and computers, ordinary humans often need a little help getting through the day. Sometimes ordinary humans wish training manuals had just the steps needed to get the job done and that's exactly what you'll find in this handy quick reference guide filled with step-by-step instructions and shortcuts for how to use Microsoft Windows 10.

Not only does this book provide a streamlined and concise learning experience, it is also an easy to use reference guide for any type of user that will help you get the job done quickly. Using this guide, you'll be able to:

- Teach yourself the essentials and latest features
- Learn how the new Windows works
- Work more efficiently with Windows 10
- Find just the tasks you need

Use the links provided in the Table of Contents at the end of this book to jump quickly to any task. Refer back to the Table of Contents to jump quickly to any other task. For example, on a kindle e-reader, slide in from the left to view the Table of Contents at any time.

Other resources I recommend for mastering Windows 10:

- Windows 10: The Personal Trainer by William Stanek
- Windows 10: Fast Start by Smart Brain Training Solutions

Both are excellent resources that will complement this book well.

2. Flying Start

Throughout this guide, where we use CLICK, RIGHT-CLICK and DOUBLE-CLICK, you can use the touch equivalents of TAP, PRESS AND HOLD and DOUBLE TAP. HOVER means to position the mouse over the designated item without CLICKING.

When working in Tablet mode, CLICK START should be replaced

with CLICK ☰ on the START screen.

This is the Windows Logo Key on your keyboard. Press this key in combination with other keys to access keyboard shortcuts. Press this key by itself to display or hide Start.

Starting Windows

1. CLICK or SWIPE UP on the starting picture.
2. If necessary, select a user.
3. If necessary, CLICK Sign-In Options and select an alternate sign-in method:

   Picture. Draw the password gestures in the correct sequence.

   Password. Type the password and then PRESS Enter or CLICK ..

   PIN. Type the PIN.

For a password or PIN, CLICK to reveal what you've typed. If your computer is used for business or has special hardware, you may have additional options for scanning your fingerprint, face or iris.

Switching Users

If your computer has multiple user accounts, you can switch to another user without having to log out. Switching users saves your work and allows another user to log in. Then when the user is finished using the computer, the user can sign out and you can sign in again and resume your work.

To switch users, CLICK START, and choose the user to switch with.

Working with Tablet Mode

When you're using Windows 10 on a tablet, tablet mode is enabled by default. With tablet mode, your device has a Start screen instead of a Start menu, app icons are hidden on the taskbar and apps open in full-screen mode. Further, the Start screen is displayed when you login instead of the desktop.

To display app icons on the taskbar when using tablet mode, CLICK START, , System, Tablet Mode. Next, CLICK Hide App Icons... setting it to the OFF position.

To go to the desktop instead of Start when you login, CLICK

START, , System, Tablet Mode. Next, CLICK When I Sign In… setting it to the OFF position.

If you don't want to use tablet mode, CLICK START, , System, Tablet Mode. Next, CLICK Make Windows More Friendly… setting it to the OFF position.

Performing Common Tasks Quickly

Programs and Features
Power Options
Event Viewer
System
Device Manager
Network Connections
Disk Management
Computer Management
Command Prompt
Command Prompt (Admin)

Task Manager
Control Panel
File Explorer
Search
Run

Shut down or sign out   >
Desktop

1. RIGHT-CLICK Start or PRESS ⊞ +X to display the tasks menu.
2. CLICK to open an item.

Tip: Like PowerShell instead of Command Prompt?
Replace Command Prompt items with PowerShell options

in the tasks menu: RIGHT-CLICK an open area on the taskbar, CLICK Properties. Next CLICK Navigation and then CLICK Replace Command Prompt with Windows PowerShell.

Locking Your Screen

Protect your work when you step away from your computer by locking your screen. Keep in mind that locking your screen doesn't end your Windows session. Instead, your device pauses the session and you resume the session by unlocking the screen.

To lock your screen, CLICK START, and choose Lock. Or

PRESS  + L.

To unlock your screen, CLICK or SWIPE UP anywhere on the

screen, enter your password, then PRESS Enter or CLICK .

Adding System Icons to the Desktop

1. RIGHT-CLICK an open area of the desktop, CLICK Personalize.
2. Select the icons to add, such as Computer and Control Panel.

Exiting Windows: Sleep, Shutdown, Sign Out

When you are done using your computer, you can end your Windows session by signing out or turning off the device. You have two options for turning off the device:

- **Sleep**   The device enters a low-power state.
- **Shutdown**   The device powers off completely.

To sign out, CLICK START, , then choose SIGN OUT.

To sleep or shutdown, CLICK START, , then choose either SLEEP or SHUT DOWN.

3. The Big Changes

Windows 10 provides a unified experience whether you are using a smartphone, an Xbox, a laptop PC, a desktop PC or a tablet PC. To sync your settings between devices, you must use a connected account and then log-in using the same account. The standard type of connected account is a Microsoft account.

It's easy to distinguish a Microsoft account from a local computer account. Microsoft accounts have a username@domainname format, such as OrdinaryHuman.Books@gmail.com. Local computer accounts just have a user name, such as OrdinaryHuman.

In the very cool department, Windows 10 supports multiple monitors and multiple desktops. Multiple monitors allow you to connect two or more displays to your device and stretch the desktop across those monitors so you can use all of the screen real estate. Multiple desktops allow you to create additional workspaces and switch between those workspaces at any time by CLICKING the Task View button. Each workspace is a virtual desktop. Although you can have as many virtual desktops as you want, each desktop uses system resources and you'll usually want to limit the number of virtual desktops.

Other big changes:

- File Explorer has replaced Windows Explorer.
- Edge browser has replaced Internet Explorer
- Settings has replaced most Control Panel functionality.
- Search has been rebuilt and now incorporates Cortana, a virtual assistant technology.

If you have a tablet or smartphone, your device will use tablet mode by default, which is different from the standard mode used by desktops and laptops. See **Working with Tablet Mode**.

4. Apps and Start

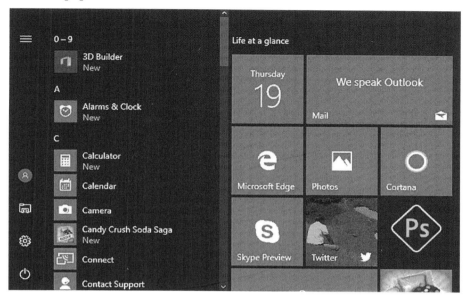

Start is split into two vertical columns with apps and options on the left and app tiles on the right. The left-side options include:

Displays account options: Change Account Settings, Lock, Sign Out. Also lets you switch to another user by CLICKING their name.

Opens File Explorer. Use File Explorer to browse your device's drives and folders.

Opens Settings. Use Settings to configure Windows on your device.

Displays power options: Sleep, Shut Down and Restart.

NOTE: The All Apps view on Start displays a sorted list of installed apps. Use Search instead of All Apps to find an app quickly. See **Searching for Apps**.

Personalizing Start

You can personalize Start by changing its default options.

1. CLICK START ( ), SETTINGS ( ).
2. In Settings, CLICK PERSONALIZATION, then CLICK START.
3. CLICK to turn on/off the Most Used or Recently Used apps lists.
4. CLICK to turn on/off Jump Lists (which show recently used files, common tasks, etc) for pinned apps whether on the Start menu or on the taskbar.
5. CLICK Choose Which Folders Appear On Start to add or remove pinned folders for File Explorer, Settings, etc.

Resizing Start

1. HOVER over the edge of the Start menu. The mouse pointer changes to the resizing pointer, showing arrows facing left and right.
2. DRAG the edge to increase or decrease the size of the Start menu.

Managing Tile Groups

Start has two tile groups, each with a default name. You can create additional tile groups.

To create a new group:

1. DRAG a tile below or to the right of an existing tile group until a new group title bar appears.
2. HOVER over the new tile group's title and then CLICK the default title.
3. Type a name then PRESS Enter.

To change the name of a tile group:

1. CLICK the name.
2. Delete or modify the existing text as appropriate.
3. Type the desired name and then PRESS Enter.

To rearrange a tile group, DRAG its title bar to a new location.

Resizing Tiles

Windows 10 has standard tiles and live tiles. The difference between the two is that live tiles display live contents that can be updated when you have an Internet connection and standard tiles display static content that isn't updated. Most tiles can be resized to small (70x70), medium (150x150), wide (310x150) or large (310x310).

- RIGHT-CLICK the tile, choose Resize, then select a size.
- Or PRESS AND HOLD the tile, TAP the options button, then select a size.

Moving Tiles

- DRAG a tile to a new position to move it.
- Or PRESS AND HOLD the tile then DRAG it to a new position.

Pinning Apps on Start

You create new tiles on Start by pinning apps.

1. On the Start menu, locate the app in the All Apps list.

2. RIGHT-CLICK the app in the list, then select Pin To Start.

Or use File Explorer to locate the item that you want to pin, RIGHT CLICK it, then CLICK Pin To Start.

To remove a pinned item:

- RIGHT-CLICK it, then select Unpin From Start.
- Or PRESS AND HOLD then CLICK the Pin button.

Searching for Apps, Settings and More

The Search box allows you to quickly search for Apps, Settings, options in Control Panel, personal files, and web sites. Initiate a search simply by typing when the Start menu is open or by CLICKING in the Search box and then typing.

The Search box is displayed on the taskbar by default, except in

tablet mode. In tablet mode, click and then enter your search text.

5. Apps and the Taskbar

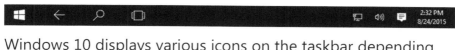

Windows 10 displays various icons on the taskbar depending on the open apps, operating mode and installed hardware. In the example, the device is in tablet mode.

Opens the Start menu or displays the Start screen.

In tablet mode, allows you to go back to the previous app or window.

In tablet mode, starts a search.

Displays or hides the task view, which allows you to quickly select an open app or window.

Displays information about network connections and allows you to access network settings.

Displays audio levels for speakers or headphones and allows you to adjust them.

Displays new notifications from Action Center. This includes alerts about security and maintenance.

When you are working in standard mode with a device running on battery power, you'll have more options, including those for working with battery-related settings and Wi-Fi.

Opens the system tray and displays icons for apps running in the background. CLICK an icon to open the related app or display an options menu. Alternatively, RIGHT-CLICK an icon to display its options menu.

> **NOTE**: If your device has Bluetooth, you'll find a related system icon. CLICK Show Hidden Icons, Bluetooth Devices, Open Settings to manage Bluetooth options. To enable Bluetooth, select the Allow Bluetooth... option. To disable Bluetooth, clear this option.

Shows remaining battery power and provides access to related settings, such as screen brightness, power & sleep settings. Click Battery Saver to enter or exit battery-saver mode.

Displays information about wireless networks and allows you to access network settings. CLICK Airplane Mode to enter or exit a protected mode that disables all network connections.

Displays the Onscreen Keyboard. With touch devices, this is a handy option to have on the taskbar.

Configuring the Taskbar

You can customize the taskbar in several ways:

- RIGHT-CLICK and then select Show Task View Button or Show Touch Keyboard Button to control whether the buttons appear on the taskbar.
- RIGHT-CLICK, select Toolbars and then select Address, Links or Desktop to control whether the related toolbars appear on the taskbar. Alternatively, select New Toolbar to choose a folder to add as a toolbar.
- RIGHT-CLICK, select Properties and then use the Taskbar Buttons options to control taskbar buttons are always combined, combined only when the taskbar is full, or never combined.
- RIGHT-CLICK, select Properties and then CLICK Customize in the Notification Area. Next, CLICK Select Which Icons Appear On The Taskbar. Use the options provided to specify which icons are displayed in the notification area.

App icons aren't displayed on the taskbar when using tablet mode. To display app icons, CLICK START, ⚙, System, Tablet Mode. Next, CLICK Hide App Icons... setting it to the OFF position.

Moving the Taskbar

By default, the taskbar is locked to prevent you from accidentally moving or hiding it. To unlock the taskbar, RIGHT-CLICK an open area on the taskbar and then select Lock The Taskbar to clear the checkmark (☑ changes to ☐).

With the taskbar unlocked, you can move it by CLICKING on it and DRAGGING.

- DRAG the taskbar to the left or right to dock it on the left or right.
- DRAG up to dock the taskbar to the top of the desktop.

After you position the taskbar lock it by RIGHT-CLICKING an open area on the taskbar and then selecting Lock The Taskbar to add the checkmark (☑ changes to ☐).

Pinning Apps to the Taskbar

1. CLICK Start to display the Start menu. Use the apps list to find the app you want to work with.

2. RIGHT-CLICK the app in the list, then select Pin To Taskbar.

Or use File Explorer to locate the app that you want to pin, RIGHT CLICK it, and then CLICK Pin To Taskbar.

To remove a pinned app, RIGHT-CLICK it and then select Unpin This Program From Taskbar.

To rearrange pinned apps, DRAG an app to a new taskbar location.

Using Taskbar Jump Lists

Jump lists show frequently or recently used files, pinned files, commonly performed tasks and other options. SWIPE UP or RIGHT-CLICK an item on the taskbar to display its jump list.

> **TIP**: Sometimes, you'll need to run pinned apps with admin privileges. To do this, RIGHT-CLICK the app, then in the jump list RIGHT-CLICK the app name. If the app can run with admin privileges, a second jump list will have a Run As Administrator option which you can select.

6. Adjusting the Volume

Whenever you are playing games, watching a movie or listening to music, you can use the audio options on the taskbar to adjust the playback volume.

Raising or Lowering the Volume

1. On the taskbar, click 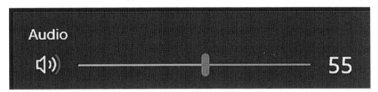 to display the Audio window.
2. Click and drag the slider to set the desired playback volume.

Muting the Volume

1. On the taskbar, click 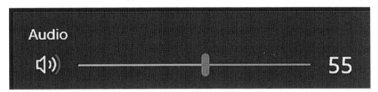 to display the Audio window.

2. Click 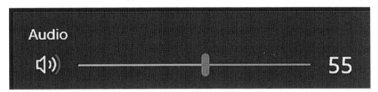 in the Audio window to mute the volume.

3.  changes to  to indicate the volume is muted.

Unmuting the Volume

1. On the taskbar, click ![mute icon] to display the Audio window.
2. Click and drag the slider to set the desired playback volume.

Alternatively, when the Audio window is open, click ![mute icon] to unmute the volume.

7. Action Center and Notifications

Open Action Center by CLICKING  on the taskbar or SWIPING IN from the right screen edge.

Action Center provides notifications about security, maintenance and system issues. Action Center notifications display icons that tell you their purpose. Alerts have warning icons.

Using Action Center

Respond to each notification as appropriate:

- CLICK or HOVER and then CLICK [icon] to expand the notification and get more details.

- CLICK or HOVER and then CLICK [icon] to close the notification.
- CLICK Clear All to remove all messages.

Using Quick Action Buttons

Quick Action buttons in Action Center allow you to perform certain actions quickly. The buttons you see depend on the type of device you are using and its hardware and can include:

- **Battery Saver** Changes system settings to reduce power consumption. Manage battery saver settings: CLICK Start, Settings, System, Battery Saver, Battery Saver Settings. Then configure the desired settings.
- **Connect** Connects to wireless devices using Bluetooth and similar technologies.
- **Location** Displays information about the current location.
- **Quiet Hours** Turns off notifications and messages until you remove the Quiet Hours option.
- **Tablet Mode** Enables or disables Tablet mode. See **Working With Tablet Mode**.
- **VPN** Provides quick access to a workplace connection over VPN.

Use Collapse to collapse the quick action buttons to a single row and show more notifications.

Use Expand to expand the quick action area to two rows and show more buttons.

Configure the button default options:

1. CLICK Start (   ), click Settings (   )
2. In Settings, CLICK System, Notifications & Action, Quick Actions.
3. CLICK each button in turn and select its default action.

8. Customizing Notifications

Icons in the notification area of the taskbar can be clicked to display related information or right-clicked to quickly access related features. By default, the notification area shows only a few icons, including Clock, Network, Notifications, and Volume. Other icons are available and can be displayed. These icons include both program icons and system icons.

Accessing Hidden Icons

To access hidden icons so that you can display related information or access related features:

1. Click  in the notification area.
2. Click or right-click the icon you want to work with.

Displaying or Hiding Program Icons

1. CLICK Start, .
2. In Settings, click System, Notifications & Action.
3. Click Select Which Icons Appear On The Taskbar.
4. For each icon that you want to display, click the related switch to On.
5. For each icon that you want to hide, click the related switch to Off.

Displaying or Hiding System Icons

1. CLICK Start, .
2. In Settings, click System, Notifications & Action.
3. Click Turn System Icons On Or Off.
4. For each system icon that you want to display, click the related switch to On.
5. For each system icon that you want to hide, click the related switch to Off.

9. Starting and Using Apps

CLICK Start, then CLICK the app tile to start an app. Or use these techniques:

- CLICK Start, scroll through the apps list, CLICK the app.
- CLICK the app shortcut on the taskbar.

Opening App Files

1. PRESS CTRL + O or CLICK File, then CLICK Open.
2. CLICK Computer, CLICK Browse.
3. Find your file. CLICK Open.

Saving New App Files

1. PRESS CTRL + S or CLICK File, then CLICK Save As.
2. CLICK Computer, CLICK Browse.
3. Select a save location, type a file name, CLICK Save.

Saving App Files in the Current Location

- PRESS CTRL + S or CLICK File, then CLICK Save.

Switching Between Apps or Windows

- PRESS AND HOLD ALT, then PRESS TAB until app is selected.
- SLIDE IN from left, then TAP the app to use.

- CLICK to open previous app.

You can also:

1. PRESS AND HOLD to show recently used apps.
2. SWIPE between them, TAP the app to use.

Using Task View to Switch Apps

1. PRESS ALT + TAB.
2. CLICK the app to use.

Close Current App

- CLICK in the upper-right corner.

Close Other Apps

1. PRESS AND HOLD ALT, then PRESS TAB until app is selected.

2. While HOLDING ALT, HOVER over app and CLICK .

You can also:

1. PRESS AND HOLD to show recently used apps.
2. SWIPE down on any app to close it.

10. Managing Apps

 Minimize app so it's hidden from view (but not closed).

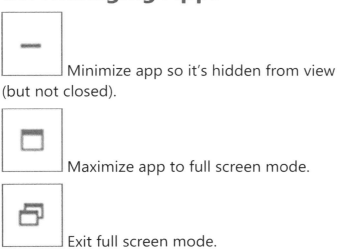 Maximize app to full screen mode.

Exit full screen mode.

Close the app.

You also can close apps using the taskbar. RIGHT-CLICK then select Close Window.

Installing Apps

1. CLICK , locate an app to install.
2. CLICK the BUY option.

Completing App Downloads

Apps you've purchased are queued to be downloaded and installed. If the download doesn't complete automatically, you'll need to restart it:

1. CLICK . Next, CLICK , then CLICK Downloads.
2. CLICK the app, then CLICK Retry.

Resizing App Windows

1. CLICK to exit full screen mode, if necessary.
2. HOVER over the left/right or top/bottom edge of the window. The mouse pointer changes to the resizing pointer, showing arrows facing left and right.
3. DRAG the edge to increase or decrease the size of the window.

Arranging Apps Side by Side

Snap is a feature of Windows 10 that allows you to arrange apps side by side or to toggle the view of an app between its standard view and snapped view.

- **+ Left Arrow**   Snaps apps to the left side of screen (or toggles to its standard view).

- **+ Right Arrow**   Snaps app to the right side of the screen (or toggles to its standard view).

- **+ Up Arrow**   Displays the app in Full Screen mode (or positions a snapped app in the upper corner so that another app can be displayed in the lower corner).

-  **+ Down Arrow** Exits Full Screen mode and returns the app to its original window state (or positions a snapped app in the lower corner so that another app can be displayed in the upper corner).

> **Tip:** Configure snap behavior: CLICK Start, Settings, System, Multitasking. Then use the options provided to manage the way snap works.

Checking for App Updates

Apps you've purchased can be updated periodically by the developer. Normally, app updates are installed automatically, if you have a Wi-Fi connection. To check for updates manually:

1. CLICK ![store icon]. Next, CLICK ![account icon], then CLICK Downloads.
2. CLICK Check For Updates.

Uninstalling Apps

1. RIGHT-CLICK on the desktop. CLICK Display Settings. CLICK Apps & Features.
2. CLICK the app to uninstall, then CLICK Uninstall.

11. Using Cortana for Search

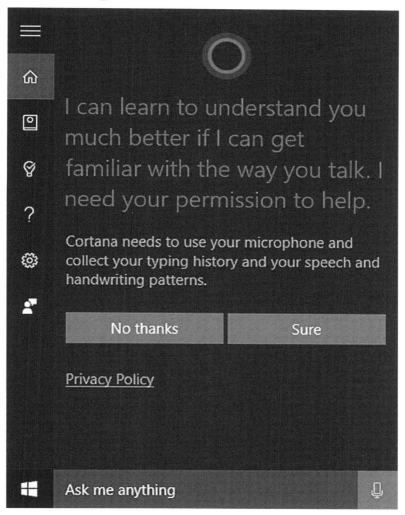

Cortana is your virtual assistant to help you with searches, give you suggestions, reminders, alerts and ideas. If your device has a microphone, you can search using your voice by clicking the Microphone (   ) button. The first time you use search with Cortana you can grant permission to collect information about your device and the way you work by clicking Sure when prompted. Otherwise, click No Thanks to close Cortana (and not collect information about your device or you).

If you enable Cortana and decide you don't want to use this feature later:

1. CLICK in the Search box. Then CLICK .
2. CLICK About me.
3. Scroll down, then click your email address.
4. In the Account dialog box, click your account.
5. CLICK Sign Out.

To search using Cortana, simply start typing when the Start menu is open or CLICK in the Search box and then start typing. Search results show related installed apps first, settings next and then apps in the Microsoft Store.

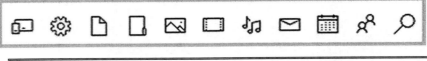

Tip: Online and web results are included by default in search results. Want results only from Settings, Control Panel, personal files, apps or documents? CLICK in the Search box and then CLICK the Apps ( ) icon, the Settings ( ) icon or the Documents ( ) icon on the Search options toolbar.

12. Using the Onscreen Keyboard

The onscreen keyboard is useful for devices without a dedicated keyboard. The keyboard opens automatically anytime you TAP in an area where text input is selected. You also can open the keyboard by CLICKING the touch keyboard button on the taskbar.

- TAP AND HOLD shift to enable/disable caps lock.
- TAP AND HOLD vowels to see common accents.
- TAP AND HOLD symbols to see related symbols.

Adding a Keyboard Button to the Taskbar

1. RIGHT-CLICK an open area of the taskbar.
2. CLICK Show Touch Keyboard Button.

Moving the Onscreen Keyboard

1. If the keyboard is docked at the bottom of the screen,

CLICK .

2. DRAG the keyboard to the desired location.

13. Creating and Managing Desktops

Window 10 supports multiple virtual desktops. Each virtual desktop provides a separate working space where you can have open apps and windows.

Creating a New Desktop

1. CLICK ___ or PRESS ___ + TAB.
2. CLICK New Desktop.
3. CLICK the desktop to use.

Opening an App on a Different Desktop

1. CLICK ___ or PRESS ___ + TAB.
2. CLICK the desktop to use.
3. CLICK Start, scroll through the apps list.
4. CLICK the app to open.

Going to a Different Desktop

1. CLICK ___ or PRESS ___ + TAB.
2. CLICK the desktop to use.

Closing a Desktop

1. CLICK ___ or PRESS ___ + TAB.

2. HOVER over the desktop thumbnail, then CLICK .

3. Any open apps or windows are moved to the previous desktop.

14. Working with Files and Folders

File Explorer has replaced Windows Explorer for working with files and folders. To open File Explorer:

- CLICK ▨ on the taskbar.
- Or RIGHT-CLICK Start, then CLICK File Explorer.
- Or TYPE File Explorer in the Search box, then PRESS Enter.

To open additional File Explorer windows:

1. RIGHT-CLICK ▨ on the taskbar.
2. CLICK File Explorer on the jump list.

Creating a Folder

1. RIGHT-CLICK an open area in File Explorer.
2. CLICK New, Folder.

Selecting Files and Folders

Select multiple items one at a time:

1. PRESS AND HOLD CTRL.
2. CLICK each item to select.

Select multiple items in a group:

1. PRESS AND HOLD SHIFT.
2. CLICK first item, then CLICK the last.

Zipping Files and Folders

1. Select items to zip. See **Selecting Files and Folders**.
2. RIGHT-CLICK, then CLICK Send To, Compressed (Zipped) Folder.
3. Type a name for the Zipped folder.
4. Press ENTER or CLICK elsewhere.

Unzipping (Extracting) Files and Folders

1. RIGHT-CLICK the zipped folder.
2. CLICK Extract All, Browse.
3. Select an extraction location, then CLICK Select Folder.
4. CLICK Extract.

Copying Files and Folders

1. Select items to copy. See **Selecting Files and Folders**.
2. PRESS AND HOLD CTRL, then drag to new location.

Moving Files and Folders

1. Select items to move. See **Selecting Files and Folders**.
2. Drag to new location on same drive.

> Tip: PRESS AND HOLD SHIFT before releasing to move to a different drive (rather than copy).

Adding Files or Folders to the Desktop

1. CLICK on the taskbar.
2. RIGHT-CLICK the file or folder after locating it.
3. CLICK Send To, Desktop (Create Shortcut).

Copying and Pasting Files and Folders

1. Select items to copy. See **Selecting Files and Folders**.
2. RIGHT-CLICK, then select Copy or PRESS Ctrl+C.
3. In the copy location, RIGHT-CLICK, then select Paste or PRESS Ctrl+V.

Cutting and Pasting Files and Folders

1. Select items to move. See **Selecting Files and Folders**.
2. RIGHT-CLICK, then select Cut or PRESS Ctrl+X.
3. In the move location, RIGHT-CLICK, then select Paste or PRESS Ctrl+V.

Renaming a File or Folder

1. RIGHT-CLICK the file or folder, then select Rename.
2. Type the new name.
3. Press Enter or TAP.

Creating and Using Desktop Shortcuts

Shortcuts help you quickly open apps, files and folders. To create a shortcut:

1. RIGHT-CLICK the app, file or folder.
2. CLICK Send To, Desktop (Create Shortcut)

DOUBLE-CLICK the shortcut to open the related item.

Deleting a File or Folder

- RIGHT-CLICK the file or folder, then select Delete.
- Or CLICK the file or folder, then PRESS DELETE.

> **Tip**: Windows 10 moves deleted items to Recycle Bin by default. To permanently delete, empty Recycle Bin. To delete a file immediately and bypass Recycle Bin, PRESS SHIFT + DELETE.

Restoring a Deleted File or Folder

If you accidentally delete a file or folder, you may be able to restore it from the Recycle Bin. The Recycle Bin is a special folder that Windows uses to temporarily store deleted files.

To restore a file or folder from the Recycle Bin:

1. If Recycle Bin is on the desktop, double-click it. Otherwise, click on the taskbar. Next, click the first **>** in the address bar, then click Recycle Bin.
2. Click the file or folder to restore.
3. On the Manage tab, click Restore The Selected Items.

The file or folder you selected is restored to its original location.

15. Searching for Files and Folders

File Explorer provides built-in search functionality. To perform a basic search:

1. Select a starting location.
2. CLICK in the Search box in File Explorer.
3. TYPE your search text, then PRESS ENTER.

Searching by Date Modified

1. Open File Explorer, then select a starting location.
2. CLICK in the Search box in File Explorer.
3. On the toolbar, CLICK Search, Date Modified.
4. Select a preset date: Today, Yesterday, This Week, Last Week, etc.
5. TYPE your search text, then PRESS ENTER.

Searching by Kind of File

1. Open File Explorer, then select a starting location.
2. CLICK in the Search box in File Explorer.
3. On the toolbar, CLICK Search, Kind.
4. Select the type of file, such as Picture, Music or Video
5. TYPE your search text, then PRESS ENTER.

Searching by File Size

1. Open File Explorer, then select a starting location.
2. CLICK in the Search box in File Explorer.
3. On the toolbar, CLICK Search, Size.
4. Select the size of the file, such as Small (10 – 100 KB) or Large (1 – 16 MB).
5. TYPE your search text, then PRESS ENTER.

16. Working with Recycle Bin

Windows 10 moves deleted items to Recycle Bin by default, giving you the option to restore deleted items to recover them if necessary. To open Recycle Bin, DOUBLE-CLICK Recycle Bin on the desktop to open it.

If there isn't a Recycle Bin icon on the desktop, add one:

1. TYPE Recycle Bin in the Search box, then PRESS ENTER.
2. In the Desktop Icon Settings dialog box, select Recycle Bin.
3. CLICK OK.

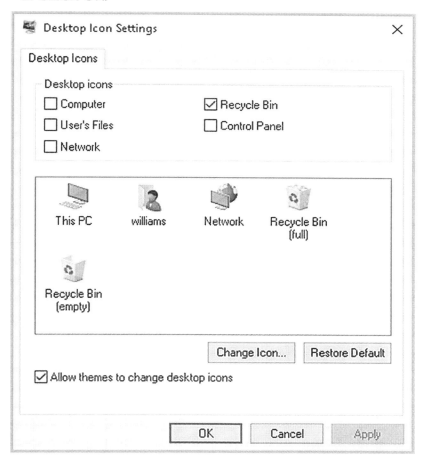

Restoring a Deleted Item

1. DOUBLE-CLICK Recycle Bin on the desktop.
2. RIGHT-CLICK item to restore, then select Restore.

Restoring Multiple Deleted Items

1. DOUBLE-CLICK Recycle Bin on the desktop.
2. Select items to restore. See **Selecting Files and Folders**.
3. RIGHT-CLICK, then select Restore.

Restoring All Deleted Items

1. DOUBLE-CLICK Recycle Bin on the desktop.
2. CLICK Mange on the toolbar, then select Restore All Items.

Emptying the Recycle Bin

1. DOUBLE-CLICK Recycle Bin on the desktop.
2. CLICK Mange on the toolbar, then select Empty Recycle Bin.

Protecting Your Files From Accidental Deletion

It's easy to accidentally delete files and folders. If you do this frequently, you may want Windows to prompt you before deleting files:

1. DOUBLE-CLICK Recycle Bin on the desktop.
2. CLICK Mange on the toolbar, then select Recycle Bin Properties.
3. Select Display Delete Confirmation Dialog.

17. Settings and Troubleshooting

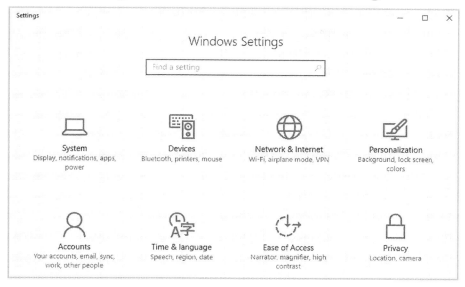

Although Control Panel remains available, Settings is the primary utility for customizing settings and options. To open Settings:

- CLICK Start (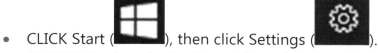), then click Settings (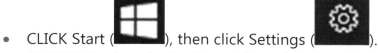).
- Or TYPE Settings in the Search box, then PRESS Enter.

When you are working with Settings, click the Home button to go back to the top-level page.

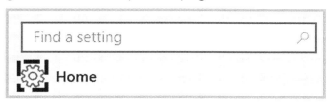

Getting Information About Your Device

1. RIGHT-CLICK on the desktop, CLICK Display Settings.
2. CLICK About to see information about your device's configuration.

Checking for Windows Updates

1. CLICK Start ( ), then click Settings ( ).
2. In Settings, CLICK Update & Security.
3. CLICK Check For Updates.

Quitting Nonresponsive Apps

1. RIGHT-CLICK Start ( ), then CLICK Task Manager.
2. RIGHT-CLICK the nonresponsive app in Task Manager.
3. CLICK End Task.

Setting the Time Zone

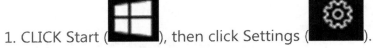

1. CLICK Start ( ), then click Settings ( ).
2. In Settings, click Time & Language.
3. In Settings, Date & Time is selected by default.
4. CLICK in the Time Zone list and then click your time zone.
5. Windows adjusts the time to the new time zone.

Using Daylight Saving Time

If you live in a location where daylight saving time applies, Windows should adjust the time automatically in fall and spring.

1. CLICK Start (), then click Settings ( ).
2. In Settings, click Time & Language.
3. In Settings, Date & Time is selected by default.
4. If set to Off, click Adjust For Daylight Saving Time to toggle the feature to On.

Checking Battery Level

1. CLICK on the taskbar.
2. The current battery level is displayed.

Changing Battery Saver Settings

1. CLICK Start (), then click Settings ( ).
2. In Settings, click System, then click Battery Saver.
3. CLICK Battery Saver Settings.
4. Use the settings provided to control battery saving options.

Renaming Your Device

1. CLICK Start (), then click Settings ( ).
2. In Settings, click System, then click About.
3. CLICK Rename PC.
4. TYPE the new name, then CLICK Next.

5. CLICK Restart Now.

Asking for Help

1. TYPE Invite Someone to Help in the Search box, then PRESS Enter.
2. CLICK Invite Someone You Trust To Help You, then follow the prompts.

18. Customizing Your Desktop and Lock Screen

The desktop and lock screen can be customized to meet your needs.

Customizing Your Desktop Background

1. RIGHT-CLICK on the desktop. CLICK Personalize.
2. CLICK the Background list, then select Picture or Solid Color.
3. CLICK the picture or color to use.
4. With pictures, CLICK Choose A Fit, then CLICK the desired fit.

Using Picture Slideshows for Desktop Backgrounds

1. RIGHT-CLICK on the desktop, CLICK Personalize.
2. CLICK the Background list, then CLICK Slideshow.
3. CLICK Browse, then select a source location.
4. CLICK Change Picture Every, then select a change option, such as 30 minutes.
5. CLICK Choose A Fit, then CLICK the desired fit.

> **Note**: Your Pictures library is the default source.

Customizing Your Lock Screen

1. RIGHT-CLICK on the desktop. CLICK Personalize. CLICK Lock Screen.
2. CLICK the Background list, then select Picture.
3. CLICK the picture to use.

Using Picture Slideshows on the Lock Screen

1. RIGHT-CLICK on the desktop. CLICK Personalize. CLICK Lock Screen.
2. CLICK the Background list, then CLICK Windows Spotlight or Slideshow.
3. If you selected Slideshow, CLICK Add A Folder and then select a source location.

Your Pictures library is the default source. To remove a source folder, CLICK it, then CLICK Remove.

Configuring Screen Timeout

1. RIGHT-CLICK on the desktop. CLICK Display Settings. CLICK Power & Sleep.
2. Under SCREEN, CLICK the On Battery and Plugged In lists and then select a turn off after value.

Configuring Sleep Settings

1. RIGHT-CLICK on the desktop. CLICK Display Settings. CLICK Power & Sleep.
2. Under SLEEP, CLICK the On Battery and Plugged In lists and then select a sleep after value.

19. Connecting to Wi-Fi

Most Windows devices have wireless adapters for establishing Wi-Fi connections.

Connecting to Public Wi-Fi

1. CLICK , then CLICK the Wi-Fi connection to use.
2. CLICK Connect.

> **Tip**: If sign-in is required, your browser should open.
> Accept the terms and CLICK the sign-in button.

Connecting to Private Wi-Fi

1. CLICK , then CLICK the Wi-Fi connection to use.
2. CLICK Connect. Note that the Connect Automatically option is selected by default.
3. Enter the network security key, then CLICK Next.

Entering and Exiting Airplane Mode

1. CLICK , then CLICK the Wi-Fi connection to use.
2. CLICK Airplane mode to toggle the mode on or off.

Airplane mode doesn't disable Bluetooth. To protect your device, you also may want to disable Bluetooth:

1. CLICK ▲, then CLICK Bluetooth Devices.
2. CLICK Open Settings, then clear the Allow Bluetooth Devices To Find... option.

Disconnecting from Wi-Fi

1. CLICK 📶, then CLICK the Wi-Fi connection.
2. CLICK Disconnect.

Forgetting a Wi-Fi Connection

Your device keeps a history of Wi-Fi connections your device has used. To remove this history and any associated network keys, access Manage Known Networks options.

1. CLICK 📶, then CLICK Network Settings.
2. CLICK Manage Wi-Fi Settings.
3. CLICK a connection, then CLICK Forget.

20. User Accounts and Security Settings

Your device can have several types of user accounts:

- **Local**   Local user accounts are created only on your device.
- **Domain**   Domain user accounts are created when your device is connected to a domain.
- **Connected**   Connected user accounts are created when you add a Microsoft account to your device.

> **Note**: Connected user accounts are connected to the Internet so that you can sync settings, documents and purchases across devices. You create connected accounts simply by adding a new or existing Microsoft account to your device.

Creating a Connected Account

1. CLICK Start ( ), then click Settings ( ).
2. In Settings, CLICK Accounts, then click Family & Other Users.

> **Note**: In a domain, Family & Other Users is renamed Other People.

3. CLICK Add Someone Else To This PC.
4. TYPE the email address or phone number of the user to add, then CLICK Next.

5. If the user doesn't already have a Microsoft account, CLICK Sign Up For A New One, then follow the prompts. Otherwise, simply follow the prompts.

Creating a Local Account

If you want to create a local account that isn't Internet-connected:

1. CLICK Start ( ), then click Settings ( ).
2. In Settings, CLICK Accounts, then click Family & Other Users.

> **Note**: In a domain, Family & Other Users is renamed Other People.

1. CLICK Add Someone Else To This PC.
2. CLICK The Person I Want To Add Doesn't Have An Email Address.
3. CLICK Add A User Without A Microsoft Account, then follow the prompts.

Changing Account Pictures

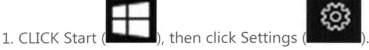

1. CLICK Start ( ), then click Settings ( ).
2. In Settings, CLICK Accounts. Your current picture (if any) is shown on the Your Info page.
3. CLICK Browse to select a picture or CLICK Camera to create a new picture.
4. Follow the prompts.

Creating a Password

All domain, local and connected user accounts can have passwords. If your computer doesn't have a password, anyone with access to your computer can sign in simply by clicking the Sign In button on the Welcome screen. They would then have access to all your data. To protect yourself and your computer, you should add a password to your account:

1. CLICK Start (   ), then click Settings (   ).
2. In Settings, CLICK Accounts, then click Sign-In Options.
3. Under Password, click Add.
4. Enter a password in the New Password box.
5. Re-enter the password in the next box, then optionally enter a password hint.
6. Click Next and then click Finish.

Creating a PIN

A pin is a numeric password usually at least 4 digits in length that provides an easier to use alternative to traditional passwords. Generally, only local accounts have pins in addition to passwords. Once you add a pin to a local account, either the password or the pin can be used to access the account.

To add a pin to an account:

1. CLICK Start (   ), then click Settings (   ).
2. In Settings, CLICK Accounts, then click Sign-In Options.
3. Under PIN, click Add.
4. Verify your identity by entering your account password when prompted, then click OK.
5. Enter a pin in the New Pin box.

6. Confirm the pin by typing it again in the next box.

7. Click OK.

Syncing Settings Between Devices

1. CLICK Start (), then click Settings ( ).

2. In Settings, CLICK Accounts, then click Sync Your Settings.

3. If set to Off, click Sync Settings to toggle the feature to On.

4. Under Individual Sync Settings, click to toggle the feature to Off for any setting that you do not want to be synced.

5. The next time Windows syncs, the settings set to On are synced with the other devices you use.

21. Securing and Recovering Your Account

Windows provides many options to help you work with your account. Some of the options help to make your account more secure. Others help you modify and maintain your account settings.

Creating a Picture Password

A picture password is a series of three gestures that you apply to a photograph. The permitted gestures are as follows:

- A click on a particular part of the picture
- A straight line drawn between two specific points
- A circle drawn in a particular area

A good picture password uses a combination of gestures and is based on a picture that has complex elements that make it more difficult for anyone to guess which gestures you might have used with various elements within the picture.

Once you add a picture password, Windows displays the photo whenever you are preparing to sign in and then you repeat the gestures to complete sign in. As the picture password is in addition to other sign-in options you've configured, you can use either the traditional password or a picture password if both are configured.

To add a picture password to an account:

1. CLICK Start ( ), then click Settings ( ).
2. In Settings, CLICK Accounts, then click Sign-In Options.
3. Under Picture Password, click Add.

4. Verify your identity by entering your account password when prompted, then click OK.
5. Windows starts the Picture Password wizard. On the Welcome page, click Choose Picture.
6. Use the Open dialog box to locate the picture that you want to use, then click OK.
7. On the How's This Look page, click and drag the picture to position it. If you are satisfied that this picture will work for creating a picture password, click Use This Picture. Otherwise, click Choose New Picture and go back to Step 6.
8. As appropriate, draw three gestures using the mouse, your finger or a stylus.
9. Repeat the gestures to confirm.
10. Click Finish.

Bypassing a Forgotten Picture Password

If you ever forget the gestures for a picture password, you can still log in.

1. On the Sign-In screen, click Sign-In Options.

2. CLICK  or to sign in with a standard password (or pin if configured).

After you sign in, you may want to review the gestures for the picture password, so that you can sign in using the picture in the future:

1. CLICK Start (), then click Settings ( ).
2. In Settings, CLICK Accounts, then click Sign-In Options.
3. Under Picture Password, click Change.

4. Verify your identity by entering your account password when prompted, then click OK.
5. Windows starts the Picture Password wizard. On the Change Your Picture Password page, click Replay.
6. Windows shows you the first gesture. Click to see the second. Click again to see the third.
7. Click Cancel.

Changing Your Password, PIN or Picture Password

1. CLICK Start (   ), then click Settings (   ).
2. In Settings, CLICK Accounts, then click Sign-In Options.
3. Under Password, PIN or Picture, CLICK Change.
4. Follow the prompts.

Registering Fingerprints for Sign-In

Fingerprints are the most secure sign in method, especially when you are using your device in an environment where someone may be able to see your password or pin. Some devices running Windows 10 come with a built in fingerprint reader. For those devices that don't you can attach an external fingerprint reader.

If your device has a fingerprint reader, you must create a pin prior to registering your fingerprint. See "Creating a Pin" for details. To configure a fingerprint for sign-in:

1. CLICK Start (   ), then click Settings (   ).
2. In Settings, CLICK Accounts, then click Sign-In Options.
3. Under Fingerprint, click Set Up.

4. Windows starts the Windows Hello Setup wizard. Click Get Started.
5. Verify your identity by entering your pin when prompted.
6. Windows Hello prompts you to scan your fingerprint. Swipe your finger across your device's reader. Repeat as necessary to finish the registration process. Generally, it takes several correct swipes to finalize registration.
7. Click Close. The next time you start your device you will be prompted to swipe your finger across the fingerprint reader to sign in.

Generally, you want to register the thumb or forefinger on your left or right hand, then remember to swipe this thumb or forefinger each time you want to sign in. If you tend to use the thumb or forefinger on either hand, you should register both the right and left thumb or the right and left forefinger.

Bypassing Unrecognized Fingerprint Swipe

If Windows does not recognize your fingerprint, you can still log in.

1. On the Sign-In screen, click Sign-In Options.

2. CLICK   or   to sign in with a standard password or pin.

After you sign in, you may want to remove the unrecognized fingerprint and then re-register your fingerprint, so that you can sign in using the fingerprint reader in the future:

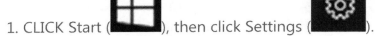

1. CLICK Start (   ), then click Settings (   ).
2. In Settings, CLICK Accounts, then click Sign-In Options.
3. Under Fingerprint, click Remove.

4. Under Fingerprint, click Set Up.
5. Windows starts the Windows Hello Setup wizard. Click Get Started.
6. Verify your identity by entering your pin when prompted.
7. Swipe your finger across your device's reader when prompted. Repeat to complete the registration process.
8. Click Close.

Changing Account Types

Users can have either standard accounts or administrator accounts.

1. CLICK Start (), then click Settings ().
2. In Settings, CLICK Accounts.
3. Under Family & Other People, CLICK the account to change.

Note: In a domain, Family & Other Users is renamed Other People.

---

4. CLICK Change Account Type.
5. CLICK the Account Type list, then select account type.

Switching Sign-In Method

1. CLICK Sign-In Options.

2. CLICK , or to sign in with a standard password, picture password or pin respectively.
3. Follow the prompts to complete sign in.

Removing Accounts

1. CLICK Start (), then click Settings (   ).
2. In Settings, CLICK Accounts.
3. Under Family & Other People, CLICK the account to remove.

> **Note**: In a domain, Family & Other Users is renamed Other People.

4. CLICK Remove, then CLICK Delete Account And Data.

Recovering Your Microsoft Password

1. CLICK   , then enter the web address as
 https://account.live.com/password/reset.
2. CLICK I Forgot My Password
3. CLICK Next and follow the prompts.

Recovering Your Local Account Password

1. Log out and sign-in with a different account.
2. TYPE User Accounts in the Search box, then PRESS Enter.
3. CLICK Manage Another Account.
4. CLICK your account you, then CLICK Reset Password.
5. Type, then confirm the new password.

22. Enhancing Security

User accounts and standard passwords are basic ways Windows helps protect your computer. Windows also includes many other features that you can take advantage of to enhance security and create multiple layers of protection to keep you and your data safe, including:

- **Security And Maintenance** A feature designed to monitor the overall security of your computer and warn you if there are problems.
- **Windows Firewall** A feature designed to prevent intruders from accessing your computer when you are connected to networks.
- **Windows Defender** A feature designed to prevent spyware and other malicious software from taking over your computer or gathering your personal information.

Checking Security Status

You can get information about the status of Windows Firewall, Windows Defender and other security features using Security And Maintenance. The related window warns you if your computer has any security issues. For example, if you turned off Windows Defender or failed to download updates to the spyware database, you'll see a related warning.

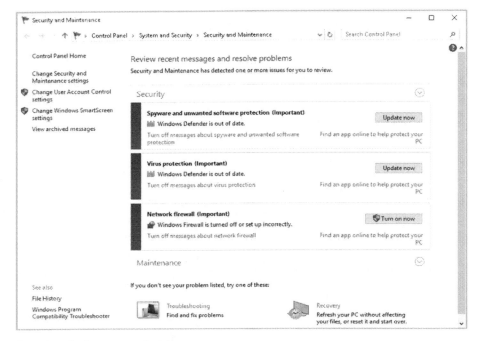

To check for security issues:

1. Type **security** in the Search box.
2. Click **Check Security Status** in the search results.
3. Review messages in the Security section.
4. Click a message button to resolve the security issue. For example, if spyware or virus protection are out of date, click Update Now. If Windows Defender or Windows Firewall are turned off, click Turn On Now.
5. Click the Security heading to view more security information.
6. Click the Maintenance heading to view additional information.

Updating the Spyware and Virus Database

Windows Defender maintains a database that contains information about spyware, viruses and other malicious software. Windows tries to update this database automatically. If Windows has problems with the update, however, you'll need to ensure your computer is connected to the Internet and then manually update the database.

To update the Windows Defender database manually:

1. Type **Windows Defender** in the Search box.
2. Click **Windows Defender (Desktop App)** in the search results.
3. If the database is out of date, you'll see a warning on the Home tab. Click Update Now.

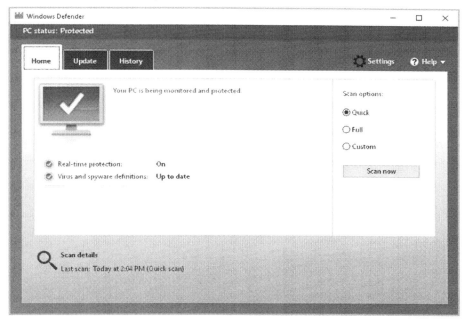

Checking Your Computer for Spyware and Viruses

Windows Defender provides real-time protection that helps to find and stop malicious programs automatically. If real-time protection is turned off temporarily, Windows will turn it back on automatically to ensure your computer is protected.

In addition to real-time protection, you should periodically scan your computer for spyware and viruses using either a quick scan or a full scan. While a quick scan checks only essential files and memory, a full scan ensures Windows Defender examines your computer, its memory and files completely.

To check your computer for malicious software:

1. Type **Windows Defender** in the Search box.
2. Click **Windows Defender (Desktop App)** in the search results.
3. On the Home tab, under Scan Options, click Quick or Full as appropriate and then click Scan Now.
4. Windows Defender will then scan your computer. The number of items Windows needs to scan determines how long the scan take. A quick scan may take only a few minutes, but a full scan can take up to an hour or more.

Turning On the Windows Firewall

Windows Firewall is used to block connections to applications running on your computer that may be used for malicious purposes. By blocking incoming connections that aren't specifically allowed for a named application, Windows Firewall enhances the overall security of your computer.

Windows recognizes three types of networks:

- **Public**   A network in a public place, or any network where you don't trust the people and devices on the network.
- **Private**   A network in at home or work, or any network where you know and trust the people and devices on the network.

- **Domain**   A network at work that uses a Windows domain where you know and trust the people and devices on the network.

Windows Firewall can be turned on or off for each type of network that you use. When Windows Firewall is on for a network, it means Windows Firewall is blocking incoming connections unless they are specifically authorized. Some outgoing connections are blocked as well. Generally, you want Windows Firewall to be turned on anytime you are using a public network and anytime any other network may not be entirely secure.

To turn Windows Firewall on or off, depending on the network type:

1. Type **Windows Firewall** in the Search box.
2. Click **Windows Firewall (Control Panel)** in the search results.
3. In the left pane of Control Panel, click Turn Windows Firewall On Or Off.
4. On the Customize Settings page, use the options provided to specify whether Windows Firewall should be enabled for each type of network available. Click Turn On Windows Firewall to ensure connections are blocked as appropriate.

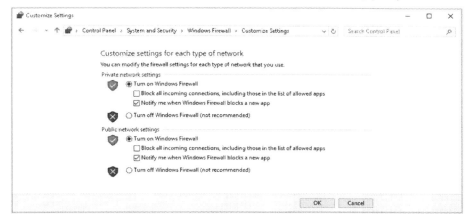

Configuring the Screen to Lock Automatically

Just as you can manually lock the screen on your computer to prevent unauthorized access, Windows can lock the screen for you as well. Automatic locking prevents unauthorized access should you forget to lock the screen when you step away from your desk or put down a mobile device.

The way automatic locking works is based on periods of inactivity. When you aren't working and your computer has been idle for a specific amount of time, such as 5 minutes, Windows locks the screen.

To configure automatic locking of the screen:

1. Type **screen saver** in the Search box.
2. Click **Turn Screen Saver On Or Off** in the search results.
3. Select On Resume, Display Logon Screen to add the checkmark (☐ changes to ☑).
4. Type the number of minutes of idle time that must pass before Windows locks the screen.

Typically, you want to use an idle value of between 3 and 10 minutes to ensure Windows locks the screen as quickly as possible.

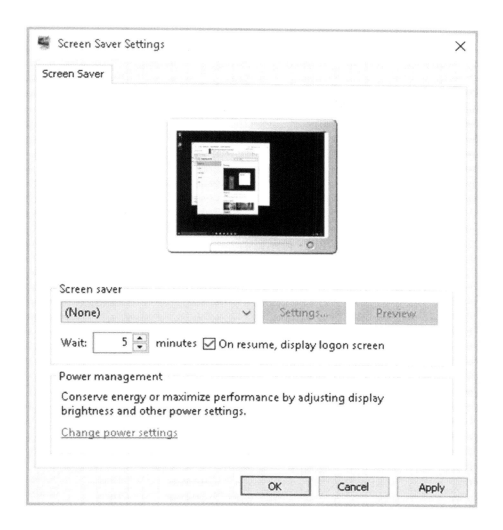

Requiring Sign-In On Wake

When your computer wakes from sleep mode, Windows is configured by default to display the sign-in screen. If Windows isn't displaying the sign-in screen on wake, you should modify the settings to require this, which helps prevent unauthorized access.

To require sign-in on wake:

1. CLICK Start (), then click Settings (   ).
2. In Settings, CLICK Accounts, then click Sign-In Options.
3. Click the dropdown list under Require Sign-In and select When PC Wakes Up From Sleep.

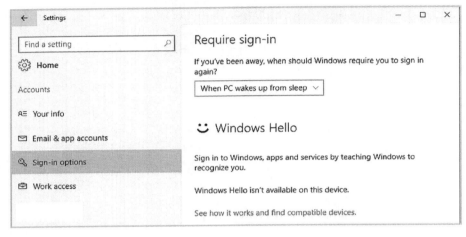

←   Settings   —   □   ×

| Find a setting | 🔎 |

🔅 Home

Accounts

A≡ Your info

✉ Email & app accounts

🔍 Sign-in options

🗄 Work access

Require sign-in

If you've been away, when should Windows require you to sign in again?

When PC wakes up from sleep ∨

😃 Windows Hello

Sign in to Windows, apps and services by teaching Windows to recognize you.

Windows Hello isn't available on this device.

See how it works and find compatible devices.

23. Maintaining Drives and Files

Your computer's hard drive is where files are stored. Use File Explorer to access files on the hard drive. To start File Explorer, click 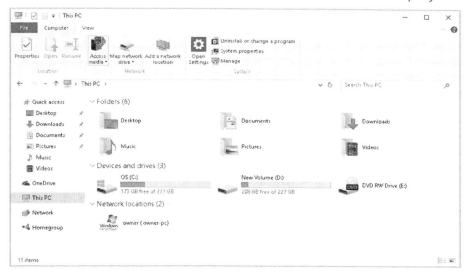 on the taskbar. You can then work with files and drives on your computer.

Viewing Drives and Storage Space

1. CLICK ▢ on the taskbar.
2. In File Explorer, CLICK This PC.
3. Folders, devices, drives and network locations are displayed.

Information about each drive is displayed under Devices And Drives. The amount of free space is depicted visually as well as by the exact amount of free space available. The total amount of space on the drive is shown as well.

OS (C:)

173 GB free of 237 GB

The bar graph is useful in helping determine the available free space at a glance. The used portion of the drive appears blue when a drive has sufficient free space but turns red when the free space becomes low.

Deleting Unnecessary Files

Windows is installed on the drive with the Windows logo:

If the free space on the Windows drive becomes low, you may notice that your computer runs slowly and your computer may run even more slowly as the drive gets closer to running out of space. For this reason, you should check the free drive space periodically and clean up unneeded files from time to time.

Generally, you want the Windows drive to have at least 10% free space. Thus, if the drive has total available space of 200 GB, you'd want at least 20 GB of free space at all times.

If necessary, you can free space on your computer by removing personal files and uninstalling programs. You also can use the Disk Cleanup app to clean up files that Windows no longer needs.

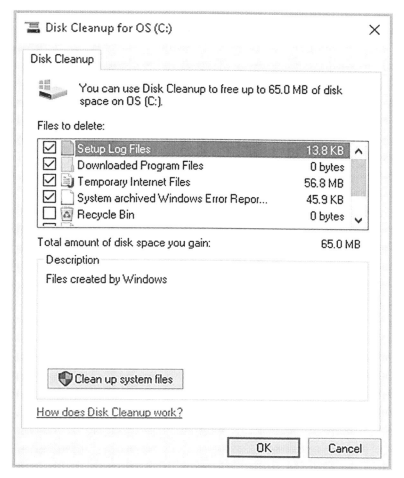

To clean up unnecessary files:

1. CLICK ![taskbar icon] on the taskbar.
2. In File Explorer, CLICK This PC.
3. Under Devices And Drives, click the Windows drive.
4. CLICK the Manage tab.
5. Click Cleanup.
6. Once Disk Cleanup initializes, you'll see the Disk Cleanup dialog box. If you want to clean up additional types of system files, click Clean Up System Files.

7. Select files to delete using the checkboxes provided (☐

changes to ☑ when a file type is selected for deletion). As you select files to delete, note the total amount of disk space you gain.
8. When you are ready to continue, click OK
9. Click Delete Files.

Checking Drives for Errors

Drive errors can cause problems that impact the performance of your computer and prevent you from saving or opening files. As discussed in "Maintaining Your Computer," Windows checks drives for errors as part of routine maintenance.

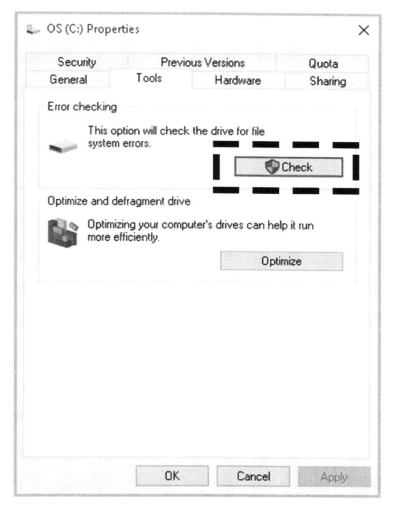

You can manually check your computer's drives for errors as well:

1. CLICK on the taskbar.
2. In File Explorer, CLICK This PC.
3. Right-click the drive you want to check, then select Properties.
4. On the Tools tab of the Properties dialog box, click Check.

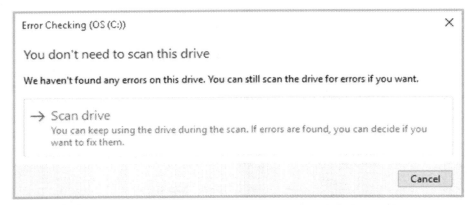

If Windows has been running maintenance checks and determined the drive has no errors, you'll see a note stating you don't need to scan this drive. Click Cancel and skip the rest of this procedure. Otherwise, click Scan Drive to have Windows check the drive. Then if Windows finds errors during the check, follow the prompt to correct them.

Defragmenting Your Computer's Drive

Your computer uses the Windows drive for storing its cache, memory paged to disk and more. Other drives may be installed as well and used by applications or for file storage. When a drive becomes fragmented, files are increasingly stored in multiple pieces instead of as a single piece, which slows overall performance anytime Windows opens or writes files. Windows itself may also run more slowly, as it reads and writes many types of files as part of normal operations.

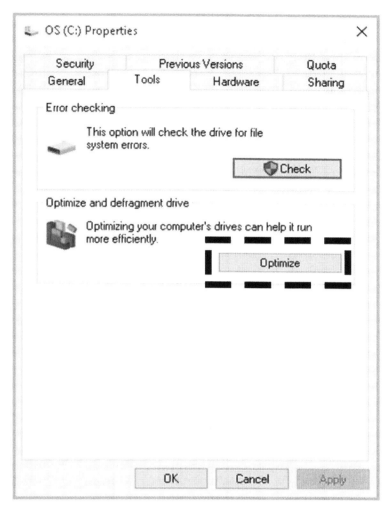

As discussed in "Maintaining Your Computer," Windows checks drives for fragmentation as part of routine maintenance. You can manually check your computer's drives for fragmentation as well:

1. Type **optimize** in the Search box.
2. Click **Defragment And Optimize Drives (Desktop App)** in the search results.
3. In the Optimize Drives window, note the last run date and the current status of drives.

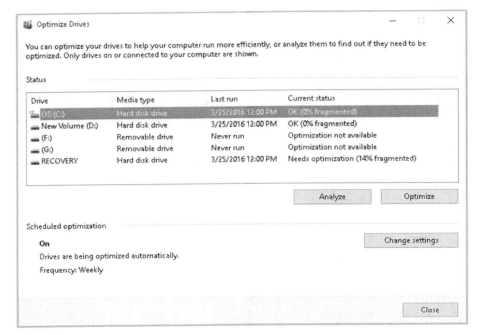

If the last run date for any hard disk drive is listed as Never Run or older than 30 days, select the drive and click Analyze. The Optimize Drives app will then check the drive for fragmentation.

If the current status of any hard disk drive is listed as Needs Optimization, the Optimize Drives app has determined that the drive has enough fragmentation to impact performance. Select the drive, then click Optimize.

If you want to try to improve overall performance, you also can have the Optimize Drives app try to optimize any drive, even if the drive isn't shown as needing optimization. Simply click the drive, then click Optimize.

During optimization, the Optimize Drives app will make several passes of the drive to try to relocate and consolidate files. This process can take as little as 3 to 5 minutes and as long as several hours, depending on the amount of fragmentation and the total capacity of the drive.

24. Keeping a File History

Windows can maintain a history of files stored in your personal folders so that you can go back to a previous version of a file if needed. When you enable the feature, the file history makes copies of files from your library folders as well as your Desktop, Contacts and Favorites folders and stores them on an external device (or network share).

Activating the File History

Windows stores the file history on an external device (or network share). Therefore, you must have a USB flash drive, external drive or available network location for saving copies of files. If you are using a flash drive or external drive, make sure there is enough space available to store copies of your personal files.

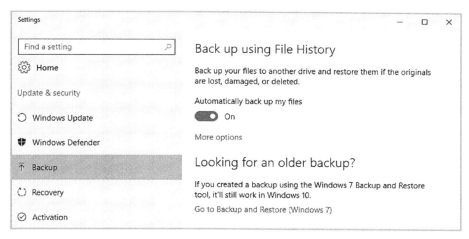

To configure your computer to use the file history:

1. Connect a USB flash drive or external drive to your computer.
2. Type **file history** in the Search box.

3. Click **File History Settings** in the search results.
4. Settings opens to the Backup page. Under Back Up Using File History, click Add A Drive, then select the device you connected.
5. If the device was used previously for file history, click Yes when prompted to confirm you want to use the drive again.
6. If another device that was used previously for file history is connected and available, you can move the existing files to the new device. When prompted, click Yes to move the files or No to skip moving the files.

Windows activates the file history and creates a copy of your personal files. If you ever need to temporarily remove the external device, you should first turn off the file history, then turn the file history back on when you reconnect the device. The exact steps are:

1. Type **file history** in the Search box.
2. Click **File History Settings** in the search results.
3. Settings opens to the Backup page.
4. Click Automatically Back Up My Files to Off.
5. You can now safely remove the external device that Windows was using to store copies of files.

When you want Windows to start creating a file history again:

1. Type **file history** in the Search box.
2. Click **File History Settings** in the search results.
3. Settings opens to the Backup page.
4. Click Automatically Back Up My Files to On.

Controlling How File History Works

With the file history enabled, Windows creates copies of files as you work. By default, the copies are created every hour, and keeps the saved versions forever. You can change these default settings:

1. Type **file history** in the Search box.
2. Click **File History Settings** in the search results.
3. Settings opens to the Backup page.
4. Click More Options.
5. Use the Back Up My Files list to specify how often copies are made. The default is Every Hour.
6. Use the Keep My Backups list to specify how long copies are kept. The default is Forever.

Restoring Files from the File History

Once you enable the file history feature, you can go back to previous versions of files stored in your personal folders at any time. For example, if you edited a file incorrectly, you could go back to a version of the file before you made the edits.

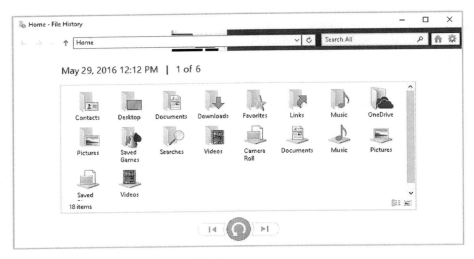

To restore a file from the file history:

1. Type **file history** in the Search box.
2. Click **File History Settings** in the search results.
3. Settings opens to the Backup page.
4. Click More Options.
5. Scroll down, then click Restore Files From A Current Backup.
6. In the Home – File History window, double-click the library or folder that contains the file you want to restore.
7. Note the date and time stamp associated with the version of the folder you are viewing. As necessary, click Previous Version ( ) to open the version of the folder you want to use.
8. Click the file you want to restore.

9. Click Restore To Original Location ( ).

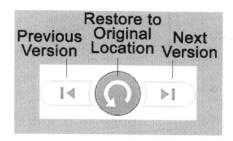

When restoring a file, Windows checks to see if the original folder has a file with this name already. If so, Windows gives you several choices. You'll be able to:

- Click Replace The File In The Destination to overwrite the existing file with the previous version.
- Click Skip This File to skip restore the file.
- Click Compare Info For Both Files to compare the file you are restoring to the existing file.

When comparing files, you can replace the file, skip restoring the file or restore a copy of the file with (2) appended to the name. In the File Conflict dialog box, click the check box beside the version of the file you want to keep. If you select only the copy, the original file will be replaced. If you select the copy and the original file, Windows keeps the original file and restores the copy of the file with (2) appended to the name.

Restoring Folders from the File History

If you ever need to restore all the files in an entire folder, you can use the file history to do this as well. Simply follow the instructions for restoring files and instead of selecting a file to restore, select a folder.

25. Maintaining Your Computer

As part of routine maintenance, Windows performs many housekeeping tasks every day to try to keep your computer running at peak performance. These housekeeping tasks:

- Check your computer's drives for errors using the Check Disk app.
- Defragment your computer's drives, if necessary using the Defragment app.
- Check for software and operating system updates using Windows Update.
- Perform security scans using Windows Defender.

Because these tasks are automated, you really don't need to run the related apps or access related features yourself. There's a catch though: Automated maintenance only works properly when you allow automatic maintenance to run and Windows has access to computer without you using the computer.

Configuring Automatic Maintenance

By default, Windows tries to run Automated Maintenance at 2:00 AM daily. Your computer must either be on and not being used by you or in sleep mode for maintenance to run. If the computer is in sleep mode, Windows can wake the computer and perform maintenance, as long as you allow this. If your computer is in use or turned off when Windows tries to perform maintenance, Windows can't run Automated Maintenance until the next time your computer is not being used.

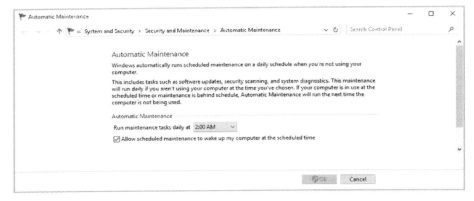

To schedule maintenance to start at a different time:

1. Type **maintenance** in the Search box.
2. Click **Change Automatic Maintenance settings (Control Panel)** in the search results.
3. Click the Run Maintenance Tasks Daily At list, then select the desired run time, such as 5:00 AM.
4. Click OK.

Running Maintenance

If Windows hasn't been able to run Automated Maintenance for more than a few days because your computer was off or being used whenever on, you may want to run maintenance manually, then let your computer work while you go to lunch or take a break. Remember, it can take several hours for Windows to complete all maintenance tasks, especially if Automated Maintenance hasn't run for several weeks.

To run maintenance:

1. Type **security and maintenance** in the Search box.
2. Click **Security And Maintenance (Control Panel)** in the search results.
3. In the Security And Maintenance window, click the Maintenance heading to expand the Maintenance panel.

4. Under Automatic Maintenance, click Start Maintenance.

Reset Your Computer

You can perform a reset to recover your computer to factory condition, which includes reinstalling a fresh copy of Windows and either removing or keeping all personal data in personal folders, such as libraries, contacts and favorites. Generally, the only time you wouldn't want to keep your personal data is when you are returning a borrowed computer, selling your computer or recycling your computer.

As a reset doesn't keep any PC settings or other configuration options, you should only perform this procedure when you are certain you want to refresh your computer and start over. Don't perform this procedure if another recovery option, such as a system restore, will work instead.

Finally, because the reset process restores your computer with a fresh copy of Windows, any Windows apps you've installed as well as any new device drivers will no longer be available. You'll need to reinstall the apps and drivers you installed after the reset.

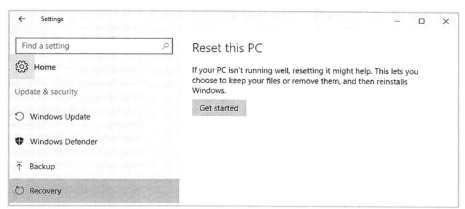

Before you reset your computer:

1. Create a backup of any personal files and documents on a USB flash drive.
2. If you downloaded device drivers and still have the installers for the drivers handy, copy the related files to the USB flash drive as well.
3. Copy any other files you think you might need to the USB flash drive as well.

To reset your computer:

1. Type **reset** in the Search box.
2. Click **Reset This PC (System Settings)** in the search results.
3. Windows displays the Settings app with Recovery selected in the left pane. Under Reset This PC, click Get Started.
4. When prompted to choose an option, specify whether you want keep your personal files or remove everything. Whether you keep files or remove everything, Windows apps will be removed and system settings will be returned to their default state.

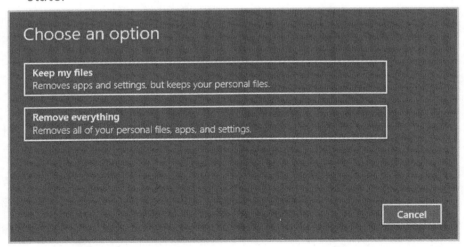

If you specified that you want to keep your files, review the list of apps that will be removed by the reset. Keep in mind that list includes apps as well as device drivers and further that the list may not be representative of all apps and device drivers that will be affected. When you are ready to continue, click Next and then click Reset.

If you specified that you want to remove files and your computer has multiple hard drives, specify whether you want to remove personal files only from the Windows drive or all drives.

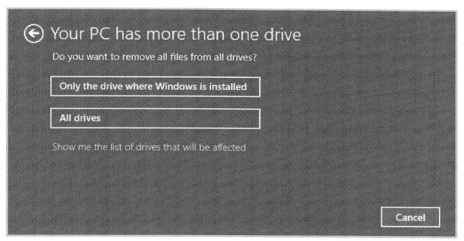

Keep in mind that simply removing the files from the computer doesn't make it so the files couldn't be recovered by someone with technical skills. For this reason, you are next asked to specify whether you want to just remove files or remove files and clean the drive(s). As stated in the prompt, if you are keeping the computer you'll usually just want to remove the files. Otherwise, if you are returning or recycling the computer, you'll want to remove files and clean the drive.

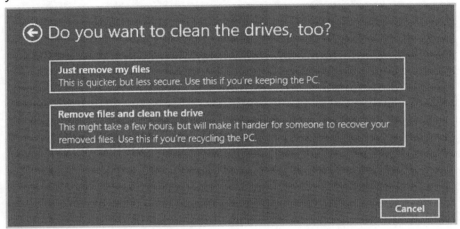

Finally, click Reset to reset the PC. The reset process will take some time and your PC will restart at least once before the process is complete.

26. Recovery and Reset

Windows makes it easy to restore your computer to working order if you run into serious problems. The preferred way to get your computer working again after a serious problem is a system restore. With a system restore, you use a previously created restore point to recover the computer to a particular point in time, such as prior to a Windows update or software installation. Another way to recover your computer is to perform a reset that restores your computer to factory condition and either keeps or removes all your personal data.

Enabling System Restore

System Restore is a feature that can be turned on or off for each internal hard drive used by your computer. System Restore is designed to preserve the state of the computer, its installed devices and programs. By default, the feature usually is enabled for the Windows drive.

System Restore doesn't preserve the state of your personal files. You protect personal files by using file history as discussed in "Keeping A File History."

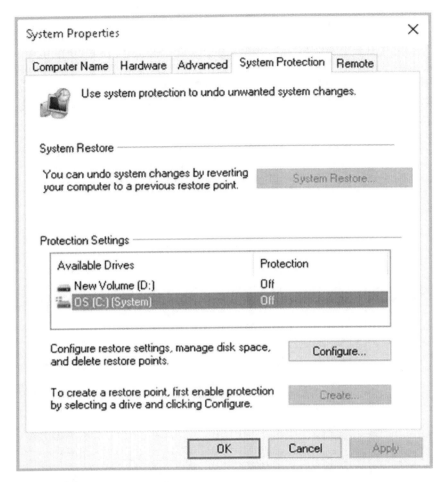

To enable system restore:

1. Type **system restore** in the Search box.
2. Click **Create A Restore Point (Control Panel)** in the search results.
3. The System Properties dialog box is displayed with the System Protection tab selected. Click the drive on which you want to enable system restore, then click Configure.
4. In the System Protection dialog box, select Turn On System Protection.

5. Drag the Max Usage slider to the left or right as appropriate to specify the maximum disk space that can be used for system protection.
6. Click OK.

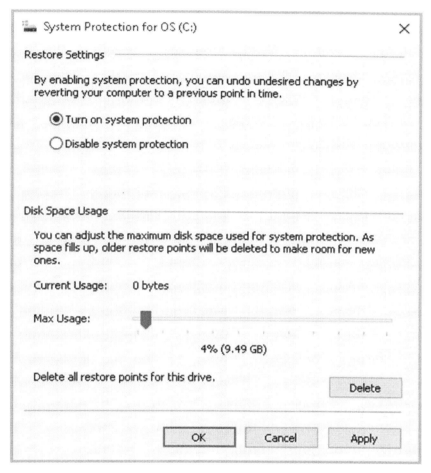

The Max Usage is expressed as a percentage of the total available space on the drive. In parenthesis, you'll also see the exact maximum storage size as well. Generally, you want to allow Windows to store at least 8 GB of restore points. As Windows uses this space, older restore points are removed to make room for new ones if necessary.

Creating Restore Points

Windows creates restore points automatically for a variety of reasons, including:

- Prior to installing updates.
- Prior to installing devices.
- Prior to installing most types of programs.

Windows also creates system restore points weekly just to be sure a restore point is available should you need one. You may want to create your own restores points periodically as well.

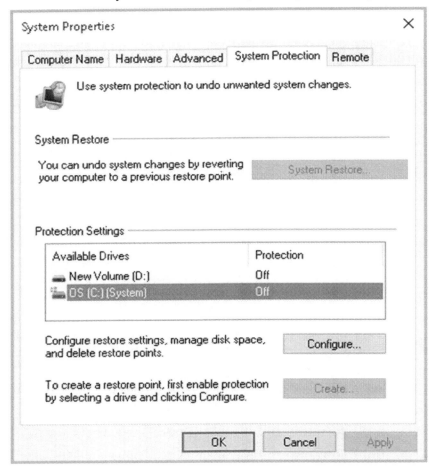

To create a restore point:

1. Type **system restore** in the Search box.
2. Click **Create A Restore Point (Control Panel)** in the search results.
3. The System Properties dialog box is displayed with the System Protection tab selected. Click Create to create a restore point for all drives that have system protection enabled.
4. Type a description of the restore point. Make sure the description helps you identify why you created the restore point.
5. Click Create. System Restore creates the restore point.
6. Click Close.
7. Click OK to close the System Properties dialog box.

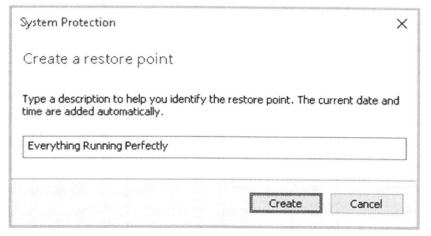

Recovering with a Restore Point

If your computer isn't working properly, becomes unstable or is otherwise experiencing problems, especially after installing a program, device or system update, you can try to fix the problem by applying a restore point. The restore point will recover your computer to a specific point in time, such as just prior to the update or device installation. As the restore only affects your computer's configuration, your personal files and documents are not affected. However, any updates to your computer that took place after the restore point, such as if you installed a program, will need to be reapplied, provided those changes were not the source of your problem.

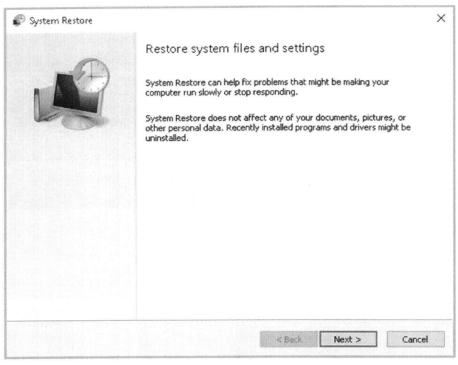

To recover with a restore point:

1. Type **system restore** in the Search box.
2. Click **Create A Restore Point (Control Panel)** in the search results.
3. The System Properties dialog box is displayed with the System Protection tab selected. Click System Restore.
4. Windows starts the System Restore wizard. Click Next.
5. Restore points are listed by date, time, description and type. Click the restore point you want to use, then click Next.

6. Click Finish. Confirm that you want to continue by clicking Yes.

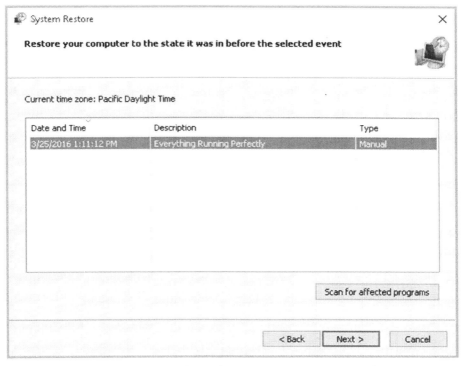

After System Restore applies the restore point, Windows restarts. When you sign in again, determine whether Windows is working normally. If Windows still isn't working properly, repeat this process and select a different restore point.

Creating a Recovery Drive

Should your computer fail to start, Windows Recovery is initiated automatically and will provide instructions for recovering your computer. Typically, this will involve using a system restore, but it may also require using either installation media. If you don't have an installation disc for your computer, you'll need to create a recovery drive instead. A recovery drive is a USB flash drive that contains the Windows Recovery environment.

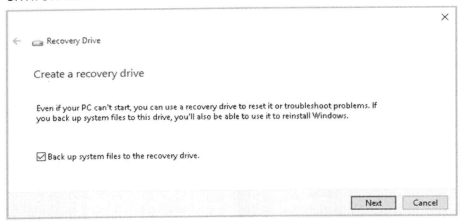

To create a recovery drive:

1. Connect a USB flash drive to your computer. As all data on this flash drive will be overwritten, this flash drive shouldn't contain any files or other data that you need.
2. Type **recovery drive** in the Search box.
3. Select **Create A Recovery Drive (Control Panel)** in the search results.
4. When prompted by User Account Control, click Yes or provide administrator credentials if necessary.
5. Windows starts the Recovery Drive wizard. Click Next.
6. Click the USB flash drive you want to use.
7. After you read the warning prompt, click Create.
8. The wizard formats the flash drive, then copies the Recovery environment, system files and other data to the drive. Click Finish.

Recovering from a Failed Start

If you still can't start your computer:

1. Insert your installation media or recovery drive, then start or restart your computer.

2. Boot to the installation media or a recovery drive.
3. In the Windows Setup dialog box, click Next.
4. Click Repair Your Computer.
5. Click Troubleshoot, then click Startup Repair. Follow the prompts.
6. If Windows Recovery is unable to repair startup, repeat this process and then select System Restore as the advanced troubleshooting option.

If a system restore isn't possible or the system restore fails several times, you may need to reset your computer:

1. Insert your installation media or recovery drive, then start or restart your computer.
2. Boot to the installation media or recovery drive.
3. In the Windows Setup dialog box, click Next, then click Repair Your Computer.
4. Click Troubleshoot, then click Reset This PC.
5. Click Keep My Files.
6. When prompted, click your account name, then type your account password.
7. Click Continue, then click Reset.

27. Commonly Used Windows Key Shortcuts

⊞ + A opens the Action Center sidebar. See **Action Center and Notifications**.

⊞ + D hides open apps to reveal the desktop or reveals the open apps that were hidden.

⊞ + E opens File Explorer.

⊞ + H opens the Share sidebar, allowing you to share a screenshot of the open app.

⊞ + I opens Settings.

⊞ + K opens the Connect sidebar for connecting Bluetooth or wireless devices.

⊞ + L signs you out of Windows. See **Exiting Windows**.

⊞ + P opens Project sidebar for selecting display options for multiple monitors.

⊞ + R opens the Run dialog box, which allows you to run commands.

⊞ + S opens the Search box so you can perform a search. See **Searching for Apps, Settings and More**.

⊞ + U opens Ease of Access Center, which you can use to make your device easier to use for those with disabilities.

⊞ + X opens the tasks menu. See **Performing Common Tasks Quickly**.

Index

Thank you...

Thank you for purchasing this book. If you enjoyed this book and learned something from it, I hope you'll take a moment to write a review. Your reviews will help to ensure I can keep writing. If you have comments for me, a wish list for additions or feedback about a topic you'd like me to write about next, contact me by sending an email to:

OrdinaryHuman.Books@gmail.com

With your support, this book will grow and grow, so be sure to look for updates periodically! To get updated content, simply delete the book off your reader and then download again at Amazon's website.

More Books...

Ordinary Human is hard at work on other books for Microsoft products. If you'd like to see a book for a particular product, let us know!

Notes...

Notes...

Notes...

Made in the USA
Middletown, DE
20 December 2016